# *An Iconic Structure*

*An Iconic Structure*

The architects and exhibit designers chosen for the National Museum team walked the German trenches and wheat fields of Belleau Wood, France. They entered Japanese tunnels and gun emplacements on Guam, Saipan, and Tinian, and they stood atop Mt. Suribachi on the exact place where the famous flag-raising took place. They experienced boot camp and lived for a few days on board ship. For Marines, the new Museum was about much more than steel, glass, and concrete. It was about capturing the resolve, spirit, and discipline of Marines.

Fentress Architects of Denver translated their experiences into a distinctive design. A gleaming central mast reaches up 210 feet, surrounded by a cone of glass. Christopher Chadbourne and Associates of Boston partnered with the architects and the Marine Corps to create a theatrical exhibit design. In 2003, general contractor Centex Corporation broke ground on 135 acres near Marine Corps Base Quantico in Virginia.

partnership was ... ,000-square-foot Mus... Marine Corps Heritage Foundation raised the funds needed for building the complex and oversaw construction with the assistance of Jacobs Facilities Inc. The Marine Corps funded the work of the architect and the exhibits designer. Design and Production, Inc., of Lorton, VA, was selected by the Marines to turn the exhibit drawings into immersive reality.

In 2008, a playground was added to the grounds, with a chapel opening in 2009. In 2010, the Museum opened three new galleries, with the assistance of exhibit fabricator Explus of Dulles, VA.

1

"Leatherneck" was a nickname given to Marines during the 19th century when they wore leather stocks on their necks. While the constrictive neckwear is gone, the image of bearing and resolve remains. This central gallery evokes bearing and resolve, but also permanence and innovation. The artifacts, vignettes, testimonials, and images in this space honor the contributions of every Marine and highlight core messages of the Museum, to include innovation and advances in technology. Suspended overhead are famous aircraft flown by Marines: a "Jenny" biplane, two Corsairs, and a Harrier "jump jet." On the ground, a Sikorsky helicopter disembarks Marines onto a Korean War position, and an amphibious tractor abuts a log wall at Tarawa. The terrazzo floor paints a picture of oceans, surf, sand, and earth, representing the expeditionary nature of the Marines, while a ship's super structure reminds us of the strong Navy-Marine Corps partnership. On the travertine marble walls, 8 large portraits of Marines and 10 famous quotes beckon the visitor to contemplate and explore.

Curtiss "Jenny"

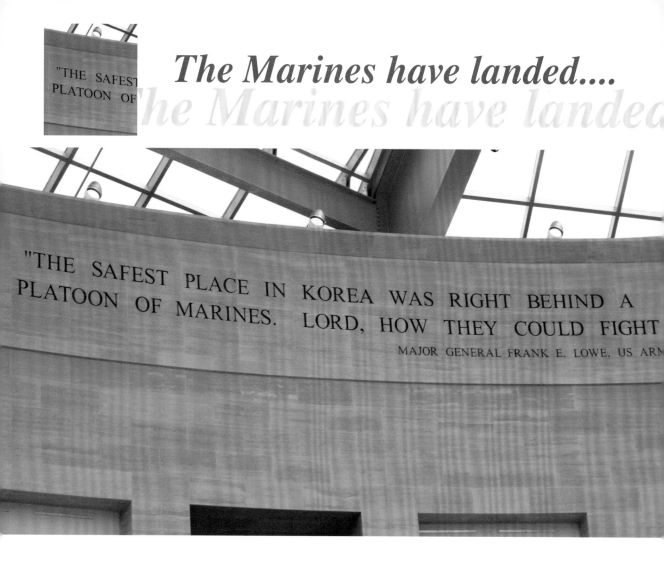

"THE SAFEST PLACE IN KOREA WAS RIGHT BEHIND A PLATOON OF MARINES. LORD, HOW THEY COULD FIGHT

MAJOR GENERAL FRANK E. LOWE, US ARM

*The Marines will never disappoint the most sanguine expectations of their country—never!*

Navy Captain Charles W. Morgan wrote this to Marine Corps Commandant Archibald Henderson in 1852, a time when Congress and the Navy were challenging the existence of the Corps. Morgan had fought alongside Marines on the USS *Constitution* in the War of 1812.

---

*The Marines have landed and the situation is well in hand.*

This dispatch is attributed to correspondent Richard Harding Davis, commenting on the Navy-Marine Corps intervention landings on Panama in 1885. It could have also applied to a dozen other landings the Marines made to protect U.S. citizens and quell disorders in the Caribbean and Central America.

---

*Come on you sons of bitches, do you want to live forever?*

Gunnery Sergeant Daniel J. Daly was the recipient of two Medals of Honor. He inspired his men by shouting this immortal battle cry on 6 June 1918 as he led his Marines in a frontal charge against the Germans at Belleau Wood in France during World War I.

*Casualties: many; Percentage Dead: unknown; Combat Efficiency: we are winning.*

Colonel David M. Shoup sent this report during the bloody battle for Tarawa Atoll during World War II, in November 1943. He led the assault forces of the 2d Marine Division against fortified Japanese defenders on Betio Island.

---

*At Iwo Jima, uncommon valor was a common virtue.*

Fleet Admiral Chester W. Nimitz, commander-in-chief of the U.S. Navy's Pacific Fleet during World War II, wrote this to the victors of Iwo Jima on 16 March 1945. In 36 days of fighting, the Marines and their Navy and Coast Guard shipmates suffered 24,053 casualties. Of those, more than 6,000 died.

---

*The value of close air support for ground troops as provided by these Maine flyers cannot be measured in words.*

Marine aviators provided sustained support to General Robert L. Eichelberger's Eighth Army in the liberation of the southern Philippines during World War II. He wrote this tribute in 1944 as Marines dropped bombs and napalm from tree-top levels.

---

*I have just returned from visiting the Marines at the front, and there is not a finer fighting organization in the world.*

General of the Army Douglas MacArthur issued this in a press release on 21 September 1950, after observing the Marines execute a regimental-sized crossing of the Han River under fire during the Korean War. The week before, they had spearheaded the amphibious seizure of Inchon.

---

*The safest place in Korea was right behind a platoon of Marines. Lord, how they could fight.*

Major General Frank E. Lowe, U.S. Army Reserve, was sent to Korea (1950-53) to evaluate the performance of front-line Army and Marine units for President Harry Truman. He often said this as he observed the Marines fighting in the Pusan Peninsula, Seoul, and the Chosin Reservoir.

---

*And they live tradition; the United States Marine bears upon his shoulders the nation's past and the nation's hopes for the future.*

Hanson W. Baldwin, Pulitzer Prize winning military editor of the *New York Times* for 40 years, wrote this about the Marine Corps in a *Saturday Evening Post* essay in October 1953. He praised the Marines for retaining their traditional values, even under the stress of enemy captivity during the Korean War.

---

*I never think of a Marine but what I think of a man who wants to do more, not less; a man you have to hold back, not shove.*

President Lyndon B. Johnson spoke these words as he presented the Presidential Unit Citation to the 5th Marines in the White House Rose Garden on 17 October 1968. The award was for extraordinary heroism against the North Vietnamese in Khe Sanh from April to June 1967.

# *Making Marines*

*Making Marines*

Whether they recall the name or not (and few forget it), all Marines remember their drill instructors.  In "Making Marines," visitors step inside the process used by drill instructors to transform young men and women into Marines.  From the home-town recruiting station to graduation, visitors are immersed in the memorable experiences that forge recruits into privates and officer candidates into lieutenants.

Listen to the thoughts of wary recruits during that first bus ride to the training depot. Stand on the famous yellow footprints and visit the barbershop where "it all gets taken away." Visitors will even have a chance to get up close and personal with their own "DI."  But the most important experience is learning how to solve problems, not on your own, but as a unit. Before graduation, try your marksmanship skills at the M-16 laser rifle range.  Remember: "Every Marine a rifleman."

6

*Team of recruits solve problem on confidence course*

*Recruits qualify on rifle range*

*Recruits negotiate weaver obstacle on confidence course*

*New Marines graduate*

# Defending the New Republic

Defending the New Republic

Outside this gallery, visitors are confronted by Continental Marines perched high atop a ship on its "fighting tops." Over 90 years of almost continuous warfare are portrayed here, from the birth of the Corps in 1775 at Philadelphia's Tun Tavern through America's costly Civil War. Marines formed armed boarding parties to serve on American ships, and they lived below deck. See the Museum's oldest artifact, an engraved powder horn used

by a Marine in 1776. Observe the cramped quarters on board a fighting vessel and learn about the difference between a smooth-bore and a rifled musket.

Muskets, edged weapons, uniforms, flags, musical instruments, and art tell the story of Marines as they helped secure America's freedom from the British, fought in the War of 1812, chased slave runners on the high seas, and participated in the Mexican War. Included is the sword presented to Lieutenant Presley O'Bannon for his actions on the "shores of Tripoli" in 1805, the earliest Marine flag from the 1840s offered by the citizens of Washington, D.C., and uniforms worn by Marines at the "halls of Montezuma."

When Civil War fractured the country, some Marines broke rank and fought for the south. Marines captured abolitionist John Brown at Harpers Ferry, and they were at Manassas. Federal Marine Corporal John F. Mackie can be seen firing on Confederate positions from a gun port on the USS *Galena*,

recreating the action that resulted in his being awarded the Medal of Honor, the first such honor for a Marine. The gallery closes with the story of the Marine who accompanied Abraham Lincoln to Gettysburg. In this first century of service, Marines won distinction fighting their country's battles around the globe and gaining popularity at home.

*Revolutionary War-era powder horn*

9

*Archibald Henderson's Virginia presentation sword*

*Royal Navy volley gun*

*Officer coatee, ca.1840-47*

*Presley O'Bannon's presentation sword*

*Presley O'Bannon's naval dirk*

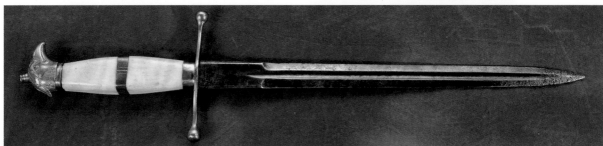

Colt M1851 Navy revolver

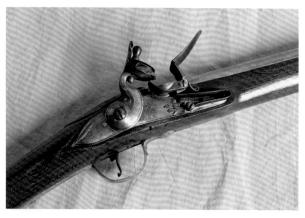
British Brown Bess musket

Civil War officer undress coat

Civil War officer full dress epaulettes

Naval swivel gun

# *Global Expeditionary Force*
*obal Expeditionary For*

The nation's last frontiers were settled by the early 1890s. American leaders turned their attention to overseas expansion, competing with other world powers. Broadening the national horizon spawned a modern and larger Navy, spurred by advocates of sea power. Marines fought enemies close to home and ancient empires across the globe and embarked on a world cruise on battleships of the "Great White Fleet." Victory in the Spanish-American War of 1898 gave the U.S. a virtual overnight empire: the Philippines, Guam, Puerto Rico. The Navy tasked the Marines to defend their busy new advance naval bases, at which American ships were supplied and serviced. Dan Daly atop the Tartar Wall of Peking in 1900 marks the entrance to this gallery, which takes visitors

to all points of the compass and travels the years 1866 to 1916.

Marines developed new capabilities. Traditional deployments as small shipboard detachments gave way to larger Marine formations. Regiments and brigades of Marines embarked for extended campaigns ashore in the Pacific and Caribbean. Visitors watch as Marines return to their campfire, having been out on watch in the Philippine jungle. Landing guns and artillery are on display, along with personal weapons used by Marines and their enemies. Uniforms, medals, and personal items give visitors a glimpse into the lives of Marines, including some who are very well known, like Smedley Butler. Overhead a Curtiss A-2 aircraft flies. On the road from Philadelphia, an early armored

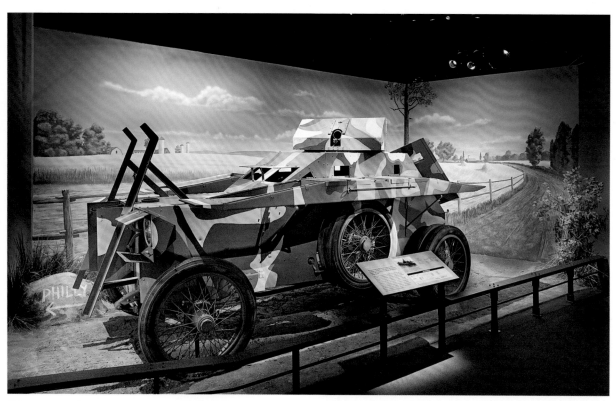

*King armored car*

*Colt USMC revolver*

*Colt M1900 pistol*

1866–1916
**CAPTURING THE HEARTS
OF AMERICANS**

car takes a break during a test run, while a Marine nearby cleans its Lewis gun. By the early years of World War I, the effects of the Industrial Revolution produced dramatic changes in the efficiency and lethality of waging war.

Closer to home, the Marines captured the hearts and minds of Americans through music. John Philip Sousa, the "March King," directed the Marine Band for many years. In the closing unit of the gallery, visitors not only see instruments from the period, they are treated to four performances of the President's Own Marine Band—up close and personal.

Medal of Honor, Captain Eli Fryer

Gold Medal awarded
by city of Nicaragua

Spanish-American War canteen

International match target rifle

# THE SPANISH-AMERICAN WAR

**"Remember the Maine!"**
*—American war slogan*

Cuba, part of the Spanish empire for almost 400 years, was fighting again for its independence in the late 1890s, a fight that many Americans supported. President William McKinley sent the battleship *Maine* to Cuban waters to protect American interests and offer assistance to some fellow Americans, where it exploded and sank on 15 February 1898, killing 260 Americans, including 26 Marines. Although no one was able to prove Spanish complicity, the U.S. linked the event to Spanish atrocities in Cuba and declared war against Spain in April.

Shipboard Marines mustered batteries to send ashore for highlighted what a beautiful American diplomat called a "splendid little war," which lasted only four months. A Marine battalion, embarked in a crowded transport, gained great public support as the first U.S. fighting force to land in Cuba, and it landed in Guantanamo Bay on 10 June where it fought Spanish regulars. The Marines then secured a position strategically located controlling water supplies, ammunition which needed fuel for its ships during the blockade of Cuba. Closer to Havana, future president Theodore Roosevelt and his Army "Rough Riders" to give its best the Spanish fleet

*Snare drum*

*Edison phonograph*

*Young John Philip Sousa's quarter-size violin*

# Marines in World War I

Marines in World War I

An American Marine and his German foe locked in hand-to-hand combat mark the entrance to this gallery. A young newsboy, closer to home, hawks his papers, with headlines that bring the visitor abreast of the news from France, held in the grip of war for several years. It is 1918, and the Marines have landed. America's young men flocked

to the colors, swelling the ranks of the Corps from 10,000 in 1916 to 75,000 in 1918. To hear the newsboy tell it, France was in trouble, and the Marines were headed for a big fight at Belleau Wood.

After a preview of battle tactics, visitors enter the French countryside, only to find themselves immersed in the battle, from the Germans' perspective. German machine gunners face the fury of the Marines' charge across the wheat field, right at them. On that single day, 6 June 1918, the Corps suffered more casualties than it had in its 143-year history. Nearby in a shell hole, Chicago *Tribune* reporter Floyd Gibbons, wounded himself, reports on the heavy fighting that would last three weeks. Beyond Gibbons, one Marine off-loads supplies from a "Tin

Lizzy" truck, while another helps a wounded Marine into the bed. Though costly, it was the Marines' first large-scale engagement that captured the world's attention.

Elsewhere in the gallery, the Museum displays many of the weapons used in this war by both sides and provides visitors with a glimpse at trench warfare, with mustard gas lingering in the air. An oral history station, with a Marine prepared for the worst standing guard, lets the participants tell you about the war and its price, in their own words.

Overhead, a fledgling Marine pilot trains for combat in a Thomas-Morse S-4B aircraft,

while a Liberty truck stands ready to take provisions to the front. The armistice went into effect on 11 November 1918, leaving 8 million combatants and 6.6 million civilians dead across Europe. The American toll was 50,000. Approximately 31,500 Marines served in France during the war and in the occupation of Germany that followed.

*Relic from battle of Belleau Wood*

Victory parade helmet

*Photo frame made from Curtiss N-9 propeller tip*

*2d Division gas mask bag*

*German gas mask*

*Marinettes take the oath*

# Uncommon Valor: Marines in World War II

Uncommon Valor
Marines in World War II

"Uncommon Valor" recalls hard-fought battles against a formidable opponent in the Pacific. The Marines entered World War II as a small expeditionary force with an unproven new mission—amphibious assault—and old equipment more suited for the jungles of the earlier "Banana Wars." But the Marines' early losses turned into later victories. These gripping stories are told with the help of tanks, artillery pieces, fighter aircraft, small arms, and the everyday "junk on a bunk" that belonged to the individual Marine. Exhibits highlight innovation in tactics, equipment, special units, Women Marines, racial integration, the Code Talkers, and Navy corpsmen.

In one immersive exhibit, visitors are told of their pending mission in a ship's briefing room just before they board a Higgins Boat for the assault on Iwo Jima. Motion, sound, and video provide a realistic experience. Close by is the flag raised on Iwo Jima and photographed by Associated Press photographer Joe Rosenthal. In a poignant display, some 6,000 small eagle, globe, and anchors and U.S. Navy and Coast Guard insignias represent the cost in human lives to take that one island. This gallery honors the sacrifices and accomplishments of America's "Greatest Generation."

*3d Raider Battalion on Torokino*

*Damaged helmet worn on Iwo Jima*

*Raider stiletto*

*Assault on Iwo Jima*

*"Gung ho" knife*

*Shadows on Okinawa*

*Sherman tank*

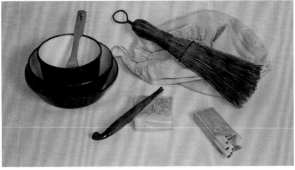
*POW artifacts*

*Marines wading ashore at Cape Gloucester*

*Cave on Okinawa*

*Second flag flown on Iwo Jima—an iconic image of the Marine Corps*

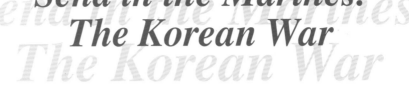

# Send in the Marines: The Korean War

Send in the Marines:
The Korean War

The "forgotten war," fought by thousands of Americans over 60 years ago against a determined enemy, is recalled in this gallery. The innovative use of helicopters to support the war is demonstrated by the presence of a Sikorsky HO3S-1 hovering overhead, but it is General MacArthur's strategic end run to attack the enemy rear at Inchon that is the first major scene. The floor shakes as visitors ride up to the sea wall with the Marines. A Pershing tank is discovered fighting in war-torn streets of Seoul. On Toktong Pass in the Chosin Reservoir visitors encounter Marines who are cold, tired, and short of ammunition. It's after midnight with the light of a full moon behind them. Visitors feel the cold; they hear the Chinese soldiers advancing up the snowy mountain, and watch while the Marines, bundled against the December weather, prepare for the next attack. They are quietly resolved to win.

In an exhibit that reflects on the uneasy "see-saw" war, visitors can board a landing craft and explore a bunker, while a Panther jet flies overhead. A sobering look into a POW cage reminds us of the high price of war.

*Medevac*

*Marching through the mountains, Chosin Reservoir*

Close-air support

*Flight scarf, Marine
Fighter Squadron 311*

*Street fighting in Seoul*

*General O. P. Smith's
helmet and M1911 pistol*

*Chosin Reservoir*

# In the Air, on Land and Sea: The War in Vietnam

In the Air, on Land and S
The War in Vietnam

Two battalions of Marines entered Vietnam in 1965, not expecting this war to become the longest war in Marine Corps history. Marines and their Allies fought insurgents and North Vietnamese forces in hamlets, urban areas, jungles, and rice paddies. In a recreated Vietnamese village, weapons and equipment used by the combatants are found, from the simple to the sophisticated: artillery, sharpened bamboo stakes, small arms, and booby traps. Stories of compassion at Hue City are described next to accounts of firefights. Wall murals and dioramas deliver stories about combat operations, significant contributions to the war, individual Marines, special units, morale, and air support.

An A-4 aircraft and the ever-present Huey helicopter represent the air war. A six-barrelled Ontos and a captured Soviet 122mm gun from Dewey Canyon hunker down realistically in the midst of the fighting.

To the sounds of a pilot talking to a Marine on the ground, visitors embark on a trip by CH-46 helicopter to Hill 881 South near Khe Sanh. Small arms fire hits the helicopter, and the crew chief instructs everyone to get out quickly. Rotor wash blows on the passengers' necks as they enter the "hot" landing zone. The space is warm; the sounds of war are all around as visitors take in the highlands of Vietnam, recreated by a talented muralist. At their feet is a dead Marine; a wounded Marine makes his way to the helicopter for evacuation in this austere and dangerous scene.

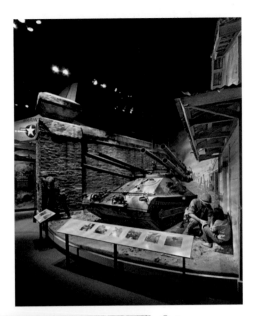

*Captain John Ripley's "advisor" uniform*

*Ontos*

*Bell UH-1E Huey*

*"Purple Foxes"*

*Chaplain's stole and damaged communion chalice*

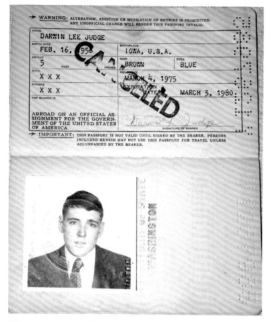

*The passport of Darwin Judge, the last Marine killed in Vietnam*

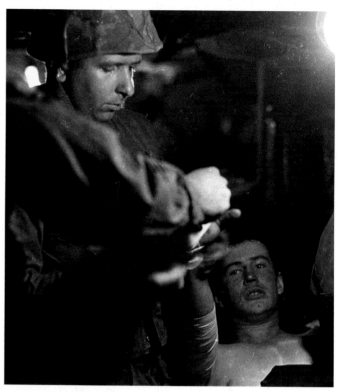

*Khe Sanh wounded*

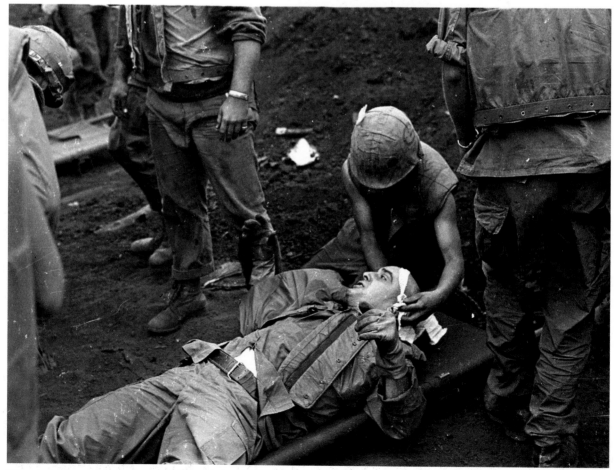

*"Four-ship" formation, Douglas F4D Skyrays*

# Combat Art
Combat Art

During World War I, years before the Marine Corps adopted an official Combat Art Program, Colonel John W. Thomason produced a powerful series of battlefield sketches that laid the groundwork that continues to define a Marine combat artist. Thomason used these field drawings to illustrate *Fix Bayonets*!, his personal recollections from the trenches of France in the "Great War."

The official Marine Corps Combat Art Program originated in 1942. Its mission was simple: Keep Americans informed of their Marines' actions overseas. Several Marine combat artists traded their World War II sea bags for highly successful careers in fine art, including Tom Lovell, John Clymer, and Harry Jackson. During the Korean conflict, Marine and civilian artists went into combat to record the experiences of leathernecks under fire. John Groth's passionately expressive ink drawings helped Americans at home appreciate the frozen hell endured by their Marines. In 1966, artists went to war in Vietnam. The Marine Corps deployed dozens of Marine and civilian artists to Southeast Asia. Since then combat artists have documented Marine experiences in such places as Lebanon, Iraq, Afghanistan, Norway, Grenada, Haiti, Kuwait, Saudi Arabia, Pakistan, Bahrain, Cuba, Somalia, and Peru. Gifted Marine Corps artists continue this tradition today wherever Marines are deployed.

The Marine Corps Combat Art Collection includes over 350 artists and nearly 8,000 pieces of fine art. Marine artists since 1946 have all been given the same guidance: Go to war, do art. The strength of the collection rests on the artists' authentic and unvarnished focus on the human condition under the most trying of circumstances.

Tarawa, 20 November 1943 *by Charles H. Waterhouse*

Fourth Marine Division at Iwo Jima *by Col Donna J. Neary, USMCR (Ret.)*

In the Bush, Chu Lai, South Vietnam
*by Col Edward M. Condra III, USMC (Ret.)*

FIRST IN
THE FIGHT~
ALWAYS
FAITHFUL~
BE A U.S. MARINE!

First in the Fight *by James Montgomery Flagg*

*Marines Today: No B*

*Combat artists and photographers deploy wherever Marines are training, fighting, or helping others.*

Marine Corps photographers assigned to Combat Camera Units capture powerful images that add depth and detail, personality and emotion to battlefield scenes. Their work also helps commanders in the field who need images to help them make real-time decisions. Since World War II, photographers armed with rifles and camera equipment have been documenting everything the field units do—from eating in makeshift mess halls to charging through combat zones. At the peak of the program during World War II, 600 Marine combat photographers contributed to documenting the war and Marine Corps life. Today, 400 personnel are assigned to Combat Camera, working in Afghanistan, Iraq, and wherever else Marines are deployed.

Their work gives visitors a glimpse onto contemporary fields of battle, precipitated by the acts of terrorism suffered by the U.S. on 11 September 2001.

The Chess Game *by Sgt Kristopher Battles, USMCR*

The Coliseum at Camp Babylon *by CWO2 Michael D. Fay, USMCR (Ret.)*

Setting Tripflares *by CWO2 Michael D. Fay, USMCR (Ret.)*

Civil Affairs Team, Iraq *by Sgt Kristopher Battles, USMCR*

# A Look Ahead
A Look Ahead

The U.S. Marine Corps and the Marine Corps Heritage Foundation intend to finish the National Museum of the Marine Corps in the years ahead. Phase 2 will include additional galleries that will take the history of the Corps from the post-Vietnam era through today's Global War on Terror. The additional 80,000 square feet will also house classrooms, a display-storage gallery on the second deck, an art gallery and combat artist studios, a large-screen theater, an administrative wing, and much more. Additionally, the Marine Corps has designated a site for a second building on the campus, which would allow the Museum to centralize all its artifact processing, storage, and preservation activities, which are presently scattered among a dozen locations on Marine Corps Base Quantico.

The public-private partnership that realized the first phase of the National Museum of the Marine Corps continues. If you are interested in supporting Phase 2, please visit **www.marineheritage.org**. If you are interested in exploring the possibility of donating artifacts to the collection, learn how at **www.usmcmuseum.org**. The job of building the Museum is a huge one. Your interest in assisting us is appreciated.

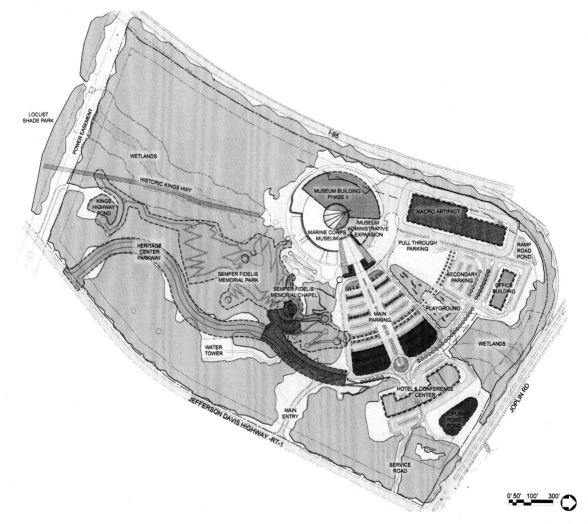